FAV

MW01035810

**Arranged for Private Prayer
in Accord with the Liturgical Year
on the Feasts of Our Lady**

●

**With a Short Helpful Meditation
Before Each Novena**

By

REV. LAWRENCE G. LOVASIK, S.V.D.
Divine Word Missionary

Illustrated in Color

CATHOLIC BOOK PUBLISHING CORP.
New Jersey

NIHIL OBSTAT: James T. O'Connor, S.T.D.
Censor Librorum
IMPRIMATUR: ✚ Patrick J. Sheridan, D.D.
Vicar General, Archdiocese of New York

(T-59)

ISBN 978-0-89942-059-2

FOREWORD

A NOVENA means nine days of public or private prayer for some special occasion or intention. Its origin goes back to the nine days that the disciples and Mary spent together in prayer between Ascension and Pentecost Sunday. Over the centuries many novenas have been highly indulgenced by the Church.

To make a novena means to persevere in prayer asking for some favor over a period of nine days in succession or nine weeks. It means fulfilling our Lord's teaching that we must continue praying and never lose confidence. This confidence is based on our Lord's words: "Ask and you will receive; seek and you will find; knock and it will be opened to you. For whoever asks receives; whoever seeks finds; whoever knocks is admitted" (Lk 11:9-10).

Many devout Catholics make novenas to Our Lady the Mother of God and Queen of Heaven. In so doing, they are following the fervent recommendation of the Church issued through the lips of Pope Pius XI: "By persevering prayer let us make Mary our daily Mediatrix, our true Advocate. In this way, we may hope that she herself, assumed into heavenly glory, will be our Advocate before Divine Goodness and Mercy at the hour of our passing."

This book is published to accommodate those who would like to make various novenas and

who would like to have them in a single volume.
A brief instruction (or meditation) precedes
each of these most popular novenas.

The purpose of this collection of novenas is
not only to provide prayers to obtain favors
from God but also to encourage people to pray
frequently because prayer, after the Sacraments, is the richest source of God's grace.

The Liturgy of the Church aids us in our
prayer-life. We can keep in touch with the
Liturgy by making a novena of prayer at various periods of the Liturgical Year. The Con-
tents are arranged clearly to help in the selec-
tion of appropriate prayers for the various
Seasons and Feasts of the Church Year.

Try to talk with God during your novena.
Absolute sincerity is most important. And as
you grow in daily reflection and prayer, you
will find yourself talking to God with much the
same ease as you would converse with a close
friend.

Use your own words in this simple, intimate
chat with God, and they will gradually become
your own personal, individual way of prayer.
You will find that the Holy Spirit is enlighten-
ing your mind and strengthening your will to
do God's Will.

Father Lawrence G. Lovasik, S.V.D.

CONTENTS

SOLEMNITY OF MARY, THE HOLY MOTHER OF GOD

(January 1)

MEDITATION

THE most sublime of Mary's privileges is her Divine Maternity. Without that Maternity, her other privileges would not exist; she herself would not exist, for she was created only to be the Mother of God.

Mary's Divine Maternity is great also because this privilege is the reason for her other privileges— her Immaculate Conception, miraculous virginity, fullness of grace, Assumption, and the spiritual maternity of all mankind. The Divine Maternity explains everything in her; without this Maternity nothing in Mary can be explained.

In her teaching concerning the union of the human and the Divine natures in Christ the Church states that Jesus Christ is God and Man, perfect God and perfect Man, and that this Divinity and Humanity are united in only one Person so that the actions of the Divine Nature or the Human Nature are the actions of one person, the Divine Person.

Since God was born of Mary, she is the Mother of God. If we could not say that she is the Mother of God for having given a body to the Son of God, then neither could we adore this Body; nor would we have been redeemed by the sacrifice of this Body on the Cross; nor would we be united to the Divinity in receiving this Body in the Eucharist.

Mary's Divine Maternity is such a sublime privilege that no creature, not even Mary herself, can understand it fully. To understand her dignity as Mother of God in all its fullness, we would have to understand fully the dignity of the Son of God whose Mother she is.

The dignity of the Divine Maternity raises Mary above all the rest of creation. As Mother of God she surpasses, in an immeasurable degree, all other creatures, Angels, and human beings. They are God's servants, but she is His Mother.

We have the sublime dignity of being children of God by adoption; Jesus alone is His Son by nature. But Mary is not the adoptive Mother of the Son of God; she is His real Mother. We can lose our Divine adoption, but Mary can never lose her Divine Maternity. God might have created a more beautiful world, more perfect people, more marvelous spirits; He could not have made anything more wonderful than a Mother of God.

Mary's Divine Maternity places her in a very wonderful relationship with the three Divine Persons. She is the loving daughter of the Father, because, before all creatures, she was predestined to be His daughter at the same moment that He decreed the Incarnation of His Son. He bestowed marvelous privileges upon her and loved her more than all other creatures together. As Mother of the Son of God, she is associated with the Father in the generation of His Son as man. With the Father she, too, can say: "This is my beloved Son in Whom I am well pleased."

Mary is the Mother of the Son of God. She fulfills the duties and enjoys the rights of a true mother. From her own flesh and blood, she formed the Body of her Son. She nourished Him, clothed Him, educated Him. She commanded Him and He obeyed. How can we ever understand the great love that bound their hearts together!

Mary is the spouse of the Holy Spirit because according to the Gospel and the teaching of the Apostles' Creed, she conceived of the Holy Spirit the Son of God, made Man. She is also called the temple of the Holy Spirit because, in virtue of her Immaculate Conception and her fullness of grace, He dwells within her in a most singular manner.

During all eternity it will be one of our greatest joys to admire the infinite love of God for Mary whose Son He willed to be, just as He is in all truth the Son of the Father. The Divine Maternity itself, more than any particular privilege, is a mark of God's unequalled love for Mary. We should rejoice with her in the happiness that filled her heart because of such love. We can ask Mary to pray to God that we return His love with some of the generosity and fervor with which she loved Him.

THE WORD OF GOD

"When the fullness of time had come, God sent His Son born of a woman … so that we might receive our adoption as children."   —Gal 4:4-5

"Shout for joy,… O daughter of Jerusalem!… The King of Israel, the Lord, is in your midst."   —Zep 3:14-15

"The Word became flesh and dwelt among us. And we saw His glory: the glory of the Only-begotten of the Father, full of grace and truth."   —Jn 1:14

"[Mary] brought forth her firstborn Son and wrapped Him in swaddling clothes and laid Him in a manger."
—Lk 2:7

NOVENA PRAYERS

Novena Prayer

I GREET you, ever-blessed Virgin, Mother of God, throne of grace, miracle of almighty power! I greet you, sanctuary of the Most Holy Trinity and Queen of the Universe, Mother of mercy and refuge of sinners!

Most loving Mother, attracted by your beauty and sweetness, and by your tender compassion, I confidently turn to you, and beg of you to obtain for me of your dear Son the favor I request in this novena: *(Mention your request).*

Obtain for me also, Queen of Heaven, the most lively contrition for my many sins and the grace to imitate closely those virtues which you practiced so faithfully, especially humility, purity, and obedience. Above all, I beg you to be my mother and protectress, to receive me into the number of your devoted children, and to guide me from your high throne of glory.

Do not reject my petitions, Mother of mercy! Have pity on me, and do not abandon me during life or at the moment of my death.

Daughter of the Eternal Father, Mother of the Eternal Son, Spouse of the Holy Spirit, Temple of the Adorable Trinity, pray for me. Immaculate and tender Heart of Mary, refuge of the needy and hope of sinners, filled with the most lively respect, love, and gratitude, I devote myself forever to your service, and I offer you my heart with all that I am and all that is mine.

Accept this offering, sweet Queen of Heaven and Earth, and obtain for me of your dear Son, Jesus Christ, the favors I ask through your intercession in this novena. Obtain for me also a generous, constant love of God, perfect submission to His holy Will, the true spirit of a Christian, and the grace of final perseverance. Amen.

Memorare

REMEMBER, O most gracious Virgin Mary, that never was it known that anyone who fled to your protection, implored your help, or sought your intercession, was left unaided. Inspired with this confidence I fly to you, O Virgin of virgins, my Mother. To you I come; before you I stand, sinful and sorrowful. O Mother of the Word Incarnate, despise not my petitions, but in your mercy hear and answer me. Amen.

Consecration

HOLIEST Virgin, with all my heart I venerate you above all the Angels and Saints in paradise as the Daughter of the Eternal Father, and I consecrate to you my soul with all its powers. *Hail Mary, etc.*

Holiest Virgin, with all my heart I venerate you above all the Angels and Saints in paradise as the Mother of the only-begotten Son, and I consecrate to you my body with all its senses. *Hail Mary, etc.*

Holiest Virgin, with all my heart I venerate you above all the Angels and Saints in paradise as the beloved Spouse of the Holy Spirit, and I consecrate to you my heart and all its affections, praying you to obtain for me from the Most Holy Trinity all the graces I need for my salvation. *Hail Mary, etc.*

Litany

LORD, have mercy. *Christ, have mercy.* Lord, have mercy. Christ, hear us. *Christ, graciously hear us.* God the Father of heaven, *have mercy on us.* God the Son, Redeemer of the world, *have mercy on us.* God the Holy Spirit, *have mercy on us.* Holy Trinity, one God, *have mercy on us.*

Holy Mary, *pray for us.* Holy Mother of God,* Holy Virgin of virgins, Mother of Christ, Mother of the Church, Mother of Divine grace, Mother most pure, Mother most chaste, Mother inviolate, Mother undefiled, Mother most amiable, Mother most admirable, Mother of good counsel, Mother of our Creator,

* *Pray for us* is said after every invocation.

Mother of our Savior,
Virgin most prudent,
Virgin most venerable,
Virgin most renowned,
Virgin most powerful,
Virgin most merciful,
Virgin most faithful,
Mirror of justice,
Seat of wisdom,
Cause of our joy,
Spiritual vessel,
Vessel of honor,
Singular vessel of devotion,
Mystical rose,
Tower of David,
Tower of ivory,
House of gold,
Ark of the covenant,
Gate of heaven,
Morning star,
Health of the sick,
Refuge of sinners,
Comforter of the afflicted,
Help of Christians,
Queen of angels,
Queen of patriarchs,
Queen of prophets,
Queen of apostles,
Queen of martyrs,
Queen of confessors,
Queen of virgins,
Queen of all saints,
Queen conceived without original sin,
Queen assumed into heaven,
Queen of the most holy Rosary,
Queen of families,
Queen of peace,

Lamb of God, You take away the sins of the world; *spare us, O Lord.*
Lamb of God, You take away the sins of the world; *graciously hear us, O Lord.*
Lamb of God, You take away the sins of the world; *have mercy on us.*

℣. Pray for us, O Holy Mother of God,
℞. *That we may be made worthy of the promises of Christ.*

L ET us pray. Grant, we beg You, O Lord God, that we Your servants may enjoy lasting health of mind and body, and by the glorious intercession of the Blessed Mary ever Virgin, be delivered from present sorrow and enter into the joy of eternal happiness. Through Christ our Lord. ℞. Amen.

OUR LADY OF PERPETUAL HELP

MEDITATION

THE miraculous picture of Madonna and Child rests on the main altar of the church of the Redemptorist Fathers in Rome. It was first in the possession of a wealthy Cretan merchant, then brought to Rome and eventually enthroned in St. Matthew's Church. For three hundred years crowds of pilgrims have journeyed far to see this picture, the source of many cures. In 1812, St. Matthew's Church was razed, and for fifty-four years the picture's location was not known. When it was found, Pope Pius IX gave it to the Redemptorist Fathers for their church on the spot where Mary first had been revered in this special manner as Our Lady of Perpetual Help.

The miraculous picture is painted like an icon. Two Angels designated as Sts. Michael and Gabriel are seen beside the Virgin's head, carrying in their veiled hands the instruments of Christ's Passion, the Cross, the spear, and the sponge. The picture was probably painted by a Greek artist of the thirteenth or fourteenth century.

Mary is invoked as Our Lady of Perpetual Help because she affords help to Christians even in all temporal needs. Although she is now enthroned in heaven, she still takes an interest in our misery and relieves our wants.

Mary brings us help especially in our spiritual needs. She is a most merciful Mother who rejects no sinner. She lovingly interests herself in our behalf and tries to reconcile us to her Son when we have sinned. She assists us in temptation. She confirms us in good and obtains for us the grace of making progress in the path of virtue, for she desires nothing more ardently than that we all become partakers of the fruits of redemption, won for us by her Son. In our efforts to reach holiness, she supports us and obtains for us the grace of perseverance. We can ask nothing of her that will give her greater pleasure or that she will grant more willingly than the grace to do good.

Above all, Mary will assist us in the hour of death, which is a crucial moment in our life because it is then that we prepare for the judgment. As the exalted Queen of Heaven she takes the souls of her faithful servants under her protecting mantle, accompanies them to the judgment seat of her Son, and there she becomes their intercessor.

Mary is still the Mother of God in heaven as she was on earth; Jesus, Who is omnipotence itself, remains her Son for all eternity. Her love for us is now even more intense and more compassionate, because she knows our misery better in heaven. She obtains gentle rest for all who are laden with trouble and pain; she gives comfort to the afflicted and healing to the sick.

Mary is our Mother of Perpetual Help, and therefore we should have an unbounded confidence in her. She can help us, for her prayer is all-powerful with God, and she will help us, for she is our Mother and she loves us as her children.

THE WORD OF GOD

"Can a woman forget her infant and be without tenderness for the child of her womb? Yet even if she should forget, I will never forget you."　　—Isa 49:15

"The wine ran out, and the Mother of Jesus ... said to the attendants, 'Do whatever He tells you.' "　—Jn 2:3-5

"Blessed are they who watch daily at my gates ... for those who find me find life and shall have salvation from the Lord."　　　　　　　　　　—Prov 8:34-35

NOVENA PRAYERS

Novena Payer

MOTHER of Perpetual Help, behold at your feet a sinner who has recourse to you and has confidence in you. Mother of mercy, have pity on me. I hear all calling you the refuge and hope of sinners. Be, then, my refuge and my hope. For the love of Jesus Christ, your Son, help me.

Give your hand to a poor sinner who commends himself to you and dedicates himself to your lasting service. I praise and thank God

Who in His mercy has given to me this confidence in you, a sure pledge of my eternal salvation.

It is true that in the past, I, miserable and wretched, have fallen into sin because I did not have recourse to you. But I know that with your help I shall be able to overcome myself. I know, too, that you will help me, if I commend myself to you. But I fear that in the occasions of sin, I may neglect to call upon you and thus run the risk of being lost.

This grace, then, I seek of you; for this I implore you as much as I know how and as much as I can: that in all the attacks of hell I may ever have recourse to you and say to you: "O Mary, help me. O Mother of Perpetual Help, do not let me lose my God."   *3 Hail Marys.*

Mother of Perpetual Help, aid me ever to call upon your powerful name, since your name is the help of the living and the salvation of the dying. Mary most pure, Mary most sweet, grant that your name from this day forth may be to me the very breath of life. Dear Lady, do not delay in coming to help me when I call upon you, for in all the temptations that trouble me, in all the needs of my life, I will ever call upon you, repeating: "Mary, Mary."

What comfort, what sweetness, what confidence, what consolation fills my soul at the sound of your name, at the very thought of you! I give thanks to our Lord, Who for my sake has given you a name so sweet, so lovable and so mighty. But I am not content only to speak your name; I will call upon you because I love you. I want that love to remind me always to call you Mother of Perpetual Help.   *3 Hail Marys.*

Mother of Perpetual Help, you are the dispenser of every grace that God grants us in our misery. For this reason He has made you so powerful, so rich, and so kind that you might help us in our needs. You are the advocate of the most wretched and abandoned sinners, if they but come to you. Come to my aid, for I commend myself to you.

In your hands I place my eternal salvation; to you I entrust my soul. Count me among your most faithful servants. Take me under your protection; that is enough for me. If you protect me, I shall fear nothing. I shall not fear my sins, because you will obtain for me their pardon and remission. Neither shall I fear the evil spirits, because you are mightier than all the powers of hell.

I fear only that through my own negligence I may forget to recommend myself to you and so lose my soul. My dear Lady, obtain for me the forgiveness of my sins, love for Jesus, final perseverance, and the grace to have recourse to you at all times, Mother of Perpetual Help.

3 Hail Marys.
(Saint Alphonsus Liguori)

— FEBRUARY —

OUR LADY OF LOURDES AND BERNADETTE

(February 11)

MEDITATION

BETWEEN February 11 and July 16, 1858, the Blessed Virgin came down from heaven eighteen times and showed herself at Lourdes to Bernadette Soubirous a little girl of fourteen years of age. On February 11, while gathering wood, Bernadette heard a whistle of wind. With astonished eyes she saw a niche in the upper part of a rock filled with golden light, and there in the midst of it stood a Lady of great beauty.

18

Her robe glowed with the whiteness of snow in the sunshine and swept in majestic folds to the ground. Her head and shoulders were framed by a white veil, which fell the full length of her robe. A blue sash encircled her waist, and its two ends, wide and unornamented, reached down in front almost to her feet. Each of her feet bore a rose of purest gold. A rosary, whose beads were white and whose cross and chain were of gold, hung from her right arm. Her hands were open, and her arms outstretched slightly in front.

In her apparitions our Lady appealed for penance and prayers for sinners. On March 25, the feast of the Annunciation, the Blessed Mother declared her name to Bernadette and to the world. On that day Bernadette made this request: "My Lady, would you be so kind as to tell me who you are?"

This is how Bernadette describes what happened in that last apparition: "Three times I asked the Apparition her name. At the third instance, she stretched out her hands, which until then she held joined, raised them, and she said: 'I am the Immaculate Conception.'" Then having completed her great message to the world, the Lady smiled on Bernadette and withdrew without further word of farewell.

Less than four years before these apparitions, on December 8, 1854, Pope Pius IX proclaimed that Mary in the first instant of her conception was preserved free from all stain of original sin through the merits of her Divine Son. At Lourdes the Virgin Mary had come to confirm the infallible utterance of God's Vicar on earth and declared herself not only immaculately conceived, but "the Immaculate Conception."

On October 30, 1867, Bernadette made her religious profession in the Convent of the Congregation of the Sisters of Nevers, France. In January, 1873, Bernadette became ill.

On April 16, about three in the afternoon, Bernadette prayed: "Holy Mary, Mother of God, pray for me, a poor sinner!" She made a Sign of the Cross, took the glass that was handed to her, twice swallowed a few drops of water, and then bending her head gently gave up her soul to her Creator.

Bernadette died, worn out with physical suffering, on April 16, 1879, at the age of thirty-six. Now her incorrupt body can be seen as she lay in death in the side chapel of the motherhouse of the Sisters of Charity at Nevers, where she lived and died as Sister Marie Bernard. Thirty years after her death her body was found in a perfect state of preservation, undoubtedly a token of love of the Immaculate Virgin Mary. She was beatified in 1925, and on December 8, 1933, she was canonized by Pope Pius Xl. Her feast day is February 18.

THE WORD OF GOD

"You have visited the earth and make it overflow; you enrich it greatly."   —Ps 65:10

"I have chosen and sanctified this place that my name may be there forever, and my eyes and my heart may be there perpetually."   —2 Chr 7:16

"I found delight in the human race."   —Prov 8:31

NOVENA PRAYERS

Novena Prayer

MARY, Mother of God, I firmly believe in the doctrine of Holy Mother Church concerning your Immaculate Conception: namely, that you were, in the first instant of your conception, by the singular grace and privilege of God, in view of the merits of Jesus Christ, the Savior of the human race, preserved immune from all stain of original sin.

Alone of all the children of Adam, you were gifted with the fullness of sanctifying grace that made you the object of a very special love on the part of God. How wonderful were the workings of Divine power to make you a fitting dwelling for the Redeemer of the world! With no tendency to evil, but with a deep yearning for the highest virtue, you glorified God more than all His other creatures. At the very instant of your conception your mind was filled with the light of God, and your will was entirely conformed to the Divine Will. You were always intimately united with God.

I thank God with you for these wonderful blessings. Help me to imitate your holiness to some degree. Your holiness was not the result of the privilege of your Immaculate Conception and sanctifying grace alone, but followed from your gift of yourself to God and your constant cooperation with His graces. Help me to be generous with God by turning to good account the graces that He ever bestows on me, and by rising promptly when I fall, with renewed confidence in His mercy.

Ever Immaculate Virgin, Mother of mercy, health of the sick, refuge of sinners, comfort of the afflicted, you know my wants, my troubles, my sufferings. Deign to cast upon me a look of mercy.

By appearing in the Grotto of Lourdes, you were pleased to make it a privileged sanctuary, from which you dispense your favors; and already many sufferers have obtained the cure of their infirmities, both spiritual and corporal. I come, therefore, with the most unbounded confidence to implore your maternal intercession.

Obtain, O loving Mother, the granting of my requests. Through gratitude for your favors, I will endeavor to imitate your virtues that I may one day share your glory.

Through your loving compassion shown to thousands of pilgrims who come to your shrine at Lourdes, and through your special love for your devoted client Bernadette, I ask for this grace if it be the Will of God: *(Mention your request).*

Our Lady of Lourdes, aid me through your prayer with your Divine Son, to be a true child of yours, as Bernadette was, and to grow daily into your likeness.

Prayer to Saint Bernadette

SAINT Bernadette, little shepherdess of Lourdes, favored with eighteen apparitions of the Immaculate Virgin Mary and with the privilege of lovingly conversing with her, now that you are eternally enjoying the entrancing beauty of the Immaculate Mother of God, do not forsake me, your devoted client, who am still in this valley of tears.

Intercede for me that I, too, may walk the simple paths of faith. Help me to imitate your example, at our heavenly Queen's request, by saying the Rosary daily and by doing penance for sinners.

Teach me to imitate your wonderful devotedness to God and our Lady, the Immaculate Conception, so that, like you, I may be blessed with the grace of lasting faithfulness and enjoy the happiness in heaven of the eternal vision of God the Father, Son, and Holy Spirit. Amen.

Prayer

GOD of infinite mercy, we celebrate the feast of Mary, Our Lady of Lourdes, the sinless Mother of God. May her prayers help us to rise above our human weakness. We ask this through our Lord Jesus Christ, Your Son Who lives and reigns with You and the Holy Spirit, one God, forever. Amen.

THE IMMACULATE HEART OF THE BLESSED VIRGIN MARY

(Sat. after the 2nd Sun. after Pentecost)

MEDITATION

ANY form of veneration of the Blessed Virgin is always directed to her person. So, too, in venerating the Immaculate Heart of Mary, we revere not only the real physical Heart of our Blessed Mother, but also her person as the source and bearer of all her virtues. We expressly honor her Heart as a symbol of her love for God and for people.

The first impulses to the veneration of the Immaculate Heart of Mary are found in Holy Scripture. After the arrival of the shepherds to the crib we read: "Mary kept in mind all these things, pondering them in her heart" (Lk 2: l9).

After Mary and Joseph found the twelve-year-old Jesus in the Temple, Scripture says: "He went down with them and came to Nazareth, and was obedient to them. And His Mother kept all these things carefully in her Heart" (Lk 2:51).

At the presentation of Jesus in the Temple, Simeon predicted: "And your own soul a sword shall pierce" (Lk 2:35). These words were verified beneath the Cross, for as the Heart of Jesus was pierced by a lance, the Heart of His Blessed Mother was transfixed by the sword of sorrow. The Heart of Jesus had its first beat in the shelter of the most pure Heart of His Mother Mary, and this most pure Heart had also received in spirit the last beat of the Heart of Jesus. If the Sacred Heart would not be without the loving Heart of His Mother in heaven, He did not wish to be honored apart from her upon earth.

In one of the first apparitions at Fatima in 1917, our Lady said that Lucy must remain on earth a while longer to spread devotion to the Immaculate Heart of Mary.

In the third apparition at Fatima, July 13, 1917, our Lady told Lucy: "Our Lord wishes that devotion to my Immaculate Heart be established in the world. If what I tell you is done, many souls will be saved and there will be peace; the war will end. . . . I ask the consecration of Russia to my Immaculate Heart and Communion of reparation on the First Saturday of each month. . . . If my requests are granted, Russia will be converted and there will be peace. . . . In the end my Immaculate Heart will triumph, and an era of peace will be conceded to humanity."

On October 31, 1942, Pope Pius XII consecrated the world to the Immaculate Heart of Mary. The same Pope consecrated Russia to our Lady in 1952. The consecration of the world was renewed by Paul VI in 1964 and by John Paul II in 1981.

Shortly before Jacinta died at the age of ten, she said to Lucy, "I have only a short time left before I go to heaven, but you must remain here below to make the world know that our Lord wishes devotion to the Immaculate Heart of Mary established in the world.... Tell everybody that God gives graces through the Immaculate Heart of Mary. Tell them to ask these graces from her, and that the Heart of Jesus wishes to be venerated together with the Immaculate Heart of His Mother. Ask them to plead for peace from the Immaculate Heart of Mary, for the Lord has confided the peace of the world to her."

In obedience to her ecclesiastical superior and her confessor, Lucy revealed a part of the secret confided by our Lady, and it concerns the devotion to the Immaculate Heart of Mary.

Pope Pius XII instituted the Feast of the Immaculate Heart of Mary in 1945, to be celebrated on August 22. Today the Feast is celebrated on the Saturday following the Second Sunday of Pentecost.

THE WORD OF GOD

"The daughter of the King enters all glorious; her raiment is made of spun gold."   —Ps 45:14

"She is the brightness of eternal light, the unspotted mirror of the majesty of God, the image of His goodness." —Wis 7:26

"His Mother kept all these things carefully in her Heart." —Lk 2:51

NOVENA PRAYERS

Novena Prayer

IMMACULATE Heart of Mary, full of love for God and mankind, and of compassion for sinners, I consecrate myself entirely to you. I entrust to you the salvation of my soul. May my heart be ever united with yours, so that I may hate sin, love God, and my neighbor, and reach eternal life together with those whom I love.

Mediatrix of All Graces and Mother of Mercy, remember the infinite treasure which your Divine Son has merited by His sufferings and which He has confided to you for us, your children. Filled with confidence in your motherly Heart, which I venerate and love, I come to you with my pressing needs. Through the merits of your loving Heart, and for the sake of the Sacred Heart of Jesus, obtain for me the favor I ask: *(Mention your request).*

Dearest Mother, if what I ask for should not be according to God's Will, pray that I may receive that which will be of greater benefit to my soul. May I experience the kindness of your motherly Heart and the power of your intercession with Jesus during life and at the hour of my death. Amen.

Petitions

IMMACULATE Virgin, conceived without sin, you directed every movement of your most pure Heart toward God and were always obedient to His Divine Will. Obtain for me the grace to hate sin with all my heart and to learn from you to live in perfect resignation to the Will of God.

Mary, I admire that deep humility which troubled your blessed Heart at the message of the Angel Gabriel when he announced that you had been chosen to be the Mother of the Son of the most high God. You considered yourself only God's lowly handmaid. Ashamed at the sight of my own pride, I beg of you the grace of a contrite and humble heart so that I may acknowledge my misery and reach the glory promised to the truly humble of heart.

Blessed Virgin, you kept in your Heart the precious treasure of the words of Jesus your Son and, pondering over the sublime mysteries they contained, you lived only for God. How ashamed I am of my coldness of heart! Dear Mother, obtain for me the grace of meditating always on the holy law of God and of seeking to follow your example in the fervent practice of all the Christian virtues.

Glorious Queen of Martyrs, during the Passion of your Son your holy Heart was cruelly pierced by the sword which had been foretold by the holy and aged Simeon. Obtain for my heart true courage and holy patience to bear the sufferings and trials of this difficult life. May I prove to be your true child by crucifying my flesh and all its desires in the mortification of the Cross.

Mary, Mystical Rose, your amiable Heart, burning with the living fire of love, adopted us as your children at the foot of the Cross, and you thereby became our most tender Mother. Let me feel the sweetness of your motherly Heart and the power of your intercession with Jesus, in all the dangers that I meet with during life, and especially at the dread hour of my death. May my heart be ever united to yours and love Jesus now and forever. Amen.

Prayer

HEAVENLY Father, You prepared the Heart of the Virgin Mary to be a fitting dwelling place for Your Holy Spirit. By her prayers for us may our souls become a more worthy temple of Your glory. Grant this through our Lord Jesus Christ, Your Son, Who lives and reigns with You and the Holy Spirit, one God, forever. Amen.

—AUGUST—

THE ASSUMPTION OF
THE BLESSED VIRGIN MARY

(August 15)

MEDITATION

THE Blessed Virgin Mary obeyed the law of *death*, but her death was rather a peaceful slumber, a gentle separation of the soul from the body. Her soul reached such a degree of love that it seemed unable to rest any longer except in the blissful embrace of the Blessed Trinity. It left her immaculate body and sped to enjoy the blessed vision of God. But soon her beautiful soul was again united to her body which lay peacefully in the tomb, and suddenly Mary stood immortal and glorified, clothed in queenly glory.

As Angels sang their hymns of praise, Mary was *raised on high* to the Kingdom of glory by God's own power. Who can tell the joy of that loving embrace whereby Jesus welcomed and admitted His own Virgin Mother to unending union with Him in the glory of heaven!

Mary's peaceful tomb had been opened by the Apostles and found to be empty. Tradition tells us that beautiful flowers filled the place where her body had once lain, and heavenly music enveloped her empty tomb. The Apostles then realized that she had been taken up into heaven, soul and body.

It was *fitting* that Mary should be assumed into heaven with soul and body. By her Assumption God honored her body that was always the temple in which He dwelt by grace. It was a gate through which the Son of God, the Divine Word, passed to earth and became Man.

It was *fitting* that Mary's holy and virginal body which gave flesh and blood to the God of all sanctity, the Victor over death, should never experience the corruption of the grave. Death and corruption are a result of original sin; but by her Immaculate Conception Mary was preserved from original sin and its effects.

Mary offered herself to suffering and her beloved Son to death for the redemption of mankind; it was *fitting* that she should be united with Him in glory.

We should rejoice that after years of suffering on earth, Mary has at last been taken to the throne prepared for her in heaven where she reigns with her Son. The Church expresses this joy on the solemn feast of the Assumption of the Virgin Mary, August 15, which is also a Holy Day of Obligation.

THE WORD OF GOD

"We know that if the earthly tent in which we live is destroyed we have a building from God, a house in heaven, not made with hands, that will be eternal."

—2 Cor 5:1

"Mary has chosen the best part, and it will not be taken away from her."   —Lk 10:42

"A great sign appeared in heaven: a woman clothed with the sun, with the moon under her feet and a crown of twelve stars on her head."   —Rev 12:1

NOVENA PRAYERS

Novena Prayer

MARY, Queen Assumed into Heaven, I rejoice that after years of heroic martyrdom on earth, you have at last been taken to the throne prepared for you in heaven by the Holy Trinity.

Lift my heart with you in the glory of your Assumption above the dreadful touch of sin and impurity. Teach me how small earth becomes when viewed from heaven. Make me realize that death is the triumphant gate through which I shall pass to your Son, and that someday my body shall rejoin my soul in the unending bliss of heaven.

From this earth, over which I tread as a pilgrim, I look to you for help. In honor of your Assumption into heaven I ask for this favor: *(Mention your request)*.

When my hour of death has come, lead me safely to the presence of Jesus to enjoy the vision of my God for all eternity together with you.

Prayer to Mary Assumed into Heaven

MARY, my dear Mother and mighty Queen, take and receive my poor heart with all its freedom and desires, all its love and all the virtues and graces with which it may be adorned. All I am, all I might be, all I have and hold in the order of nature as well as of grace, I have received from God through your loving intercession, my Lady and Queen. Into your sovereign hands I entrust all, that it may be returned to its noble origin.

Mary, Queen of every heart, accept all that I am and bind me to you with the bonds of love, that I may be yours forever, and may be able to say in all truth: "I belong to Jesus through Mary."

My Mother, assumed into heaven, I love you. Give me a greater love for Jesus and for you.

Mary, Assumed into Heaven and Queen of the Universe, ever-Virgin Mother of God, obtain peace and salvation for us through your prayers, for you have given birth to Christ the Lord, the Savior of all mankind.

Prayer

ALMIGHTY, ever-living God, You raised to eternal glory the body and soul of the immaculate Virgin Mary, Mother of Your Son. Grant that our minds may always be directed heavenward and that we may deserve to share in her glory.

OUR LADY OF SORROWS

(September 15)

MEDITATION

THE seven Sorrows of the Blessed Virgin Mary that have made the strongest appeal to devotion are: the prophecy of Simeon, the flight into Egypt, the three days' loss of Jesus, the meeting with Jesus carrying His Cross, His Death on Calvary, His being taken down from the Cross, and His burial in the tomb.

Simeon foretold to the Mother the opposition the Redeemer would arouse. When she offered her forty-day-old Child to God in the Temple, he said, "This Child is destined for the fall and for the rise of many in Israel, and for a sign that shall be contradicted. And your own soul a sword shall pierce" (Lk 2:34-35).

Mary's sorrow on Calvary was deeper than any sorrow ever felt on earth, for no mother in all the world had a heart as tender as the Heart of the Mother of God. As there was no love like her love, there was no sorrow like her sorrow. She bore her sufferings for us that we might enjoy the graces of Redemption. She suffered willingly in order to prove her love for us, for true love is proved by sacrifice.

It was not because she was the Mother of God that Mary could bear her sorrows, but because she saw things from His point of view and not from her own—or rather, she had made His point of view hers. We should do the same. The Mother of Sorrows will be on hand to help us.

Devotion to the Sorrows of Mary is the source of great graces because it leads into the depths of the Heart of Christ. If we think frequently of the false pleasures of this world, we shall embrace patiently the sorrows and sufferings of this life, and we shall be penetrated with a sorrow for sin.

The Church urges us to give ourselves over to the love of Mary completely and bear our cross patiently with the Mother of Sorrows. She earnestly wants to help us to bear our daily crosses because it was on Calvary that her dying Son entrusted us to her care. It was His last Will that she should be our Mother. It was also His last Will that we love His Mother as He did.

THE WORD OF GOD

"This Child is destined for the fall and for the rise of many in Israel, and for a sign that shall be contradicted.

And your own soul a sword shall pierce, that the thoughts of many hearts may be revealed." —Lk 2:34-35

"His Mother said to [Jesus]: 'Son, why have You done this to us? Behold, Your father and I have been anxiously searching for You.' " —Lk 2:48

"All you who pass by the way, look and see whether there is any sorrow like my sorrow." —Lam 1:12

NOVENA PRAYERS

Novena Prayer

M OST holy and afflicted Virgin, Mother of Sorrows and Queen of Martyrs! You stood motionless at the foot of the Cross beneath your dying Son. Through the sword of grief which pierced you then, through the unceasing suffering of your life of sorrow, and the bliss which now fully repays you for your past trials and afflictions, look upon me with a mother's tenderness and have pity on me, as I pray before you to venerate your sorrows, and place my request with childlike confidence in the sanctuary of your wounded Heart.

I beg of you to present to Jesus Christ, in union with the infinite merits of His Passion and Death, your sufferings at the foot of the Cross, and through the power of both, to grant my request: *(Mention your request).*

To whom shall I turn in my needs and miseries, if not to you, Mother of mercy? You drank so deeply of the chalice of your Son that you can sympathize with the sufferings of those who are still in this valley of tears.

Offer to our Divine Savior the sufferings He bore on the Cross that the memory of them may draw His mercy upon me, a sinner. Refuge of sinners and hope of all mankind, accept my petition and grant it, if it be according to the Will of God.

Lord Jesus Christ, I offer You the merits of Mary, Your Mother and ours, as she stood beneath the Cross, in order that by her loving intercession I may obtain the happy fruits of Your Passion and Death.

Offering

MARY, most holy Virgin and Queen of Martyrs, accept the sincere homage of my childlike love. Into your heart, pierced by so many swords, welcome my poor soul. Receive it as the companion of your sorrows at the foot of the Cross, on which Jesus died for the redemption of the world.

With you, sorrowful Virgin, I will gladly suffer all the trials, sufferings, and afflictions which it shall please our Lord to send me. I offer them all to you in memory of your sorrows so that every thought of my mind and every beat of my heart may be an act of compassion and of love for you.

Dearest Mother, have pity on me, reconcile me to your Divine Son Jesus, keep me in His grace, and assist me in my last agony, so that I may meet you in heaven together with your loving Son.

Hymn — Stabat Mater

AT the Cross her station
keeping,
Stood the mournful Mother
weeping,
Close to Jesus to the last.
Through her heart, His sorrow sharing,
All His bitter anguish bear-
ing,
Lo, the piercing sword has
passed!

O, how sad and sore dis-
tressed,
Was that Mother highly
blessed
Of the sole-begotten One.
Christ above in torment
hangs,
She beneath beholds the
pangs
Of her dying glorious Son.

Is there one who would not
weep
'Whelmed in miseries so
deep
Christ's dear Mother to behold?
Can the human heart re-
frain
From partaking in the pain,
In that Mother's pain un-
told?

Bruised, derided, cursed,
defiled,
She beheld her tender
Child,
All with bloody scourges
rent.
For the sins of His own na-
tion

Saw Him hang in desola-
tion
Till His Spirit forth He sent.

O sweet Mother! fount of
love,
Touch my spirit from
above,
Make my heart with yours
accord.
Make me feel as you have
felt.
Make my soul to glow and
melt
With the love of Christ, my
Lord.

Holy Mother, pierce me
through.
In my heart each wound
renew
Of my Savior crucified.
Let me share with you His
pain,
Who for all our sins was
slain,
Who for me in torments
died.

Let me mingle tears with
you,
Mourning Him Who
mourned for me,
All the days that I may live.
By the Cross with you to
stay,
There with you to weep and
pray,
Is all I ask of you to give.

Virgin of all virgins blest!
Listen to my fond request:
Let me share your grief Di-
vine.

Let me, to my latest breath,
In my body bear the death
Of your dying Son Divine.

Wounded with his every wound,
Steep my soul till it has swooned
In His very Blood away.

Be to me, O Virgin, nigh,
Lest in flames I burn and die,
In His awe-full judgment day.

Christ, when You shall call me hence,
Be Your Mother my defense,
Be Your Cross my victory.

While my body here decays,
May my soul Your goodness praise,
Safe in heaven eternally.
Amen. Alleluia.

Prayer

FATHER, it was Your Will that the compassionate Mother of Your Son should stand near the Cross on which He was glorified. Grant that Your Church, having shared in Christ's Passion, may also participate in His Resurrection. We ask this through our Lord, Jesus Christ, Your Son, Who lives and reigns with You and the Holy Spirit, one God, forever. Amen.

Prayer after the Rosary

(To be used at the end of pages 44-47.)

LET us pray. God, Whose only-begotten Son by His Life, Death, and Resurrection obtained for us the rewards of eternal salvation grant, we beg of You, that meditating upon these mysteries in the most Holy Rosary of the Blessed Virgin Mary, we may both imitate what they contain and obtain what they promise. Through Christ our Lord. ℟. *Amen.*

—OCTOBER—

ROSARY NOVENA

(Our Lady of the Rosary, October 7)

MEDITATION

THE Rosary is a favorite means of devotion to the Blessed Virgin Mary, recommended by the Popes over many centuries. It consists of various elements:

a) *Contemplation,* in union with Mary, of a series of Mysteries of Salvation, distributed into four cycles. These Mysteries express the joy of the Messianic times, events from Christ's Public Ministry called Mysteries of Light or Luminous Mysteries,* the suffering of Christ, and the glory of the Risen

---

* Suggested by Pope John Paul II in his Apostolic Letter of Oct. 16, 2002, entitled *The Rosary of the Virgin Mary.*

Lord which fills the Church. This contemplation by its very nature encourages practical reflection and provides norms for living.

b) *The Lord's Prayer*, which by reason of its immense value is at the basis of Christian prayer and ennobles that prayer in its various expressions.

c) The litany-like succession of the *Hail Mary*, which is made up of the Angel's greeting to the Virgin (Lk 1:28) and of Elizabeth's greeting (Lk 1:42), followed by the Church's own prayer. The continued series of Hail Marys is the special characteristic of the Rosary, and their number (200) is divided into decades attached to the individual mysteries.

d) The doxology *Glory be to the Father* concludes the prayer with the glorifying of God Who is One and Three, from Whom, through Whom, and in Whom all things have their being (Rom 11:36).

In her sixth and last apparition at Fatima, October 13, 1917, the Blessed Virgin insisted on the recitation of the Rosary as a powerful means for the conversion of Russia and for peace in the world. When Lucy asked, "Who are you and what do you want?" Our Lady replied: "I am the Lady of the Rosary, and I have come to warn the faithful to amend their lives and ask pardon for their sins. They must not continue to offend our Lord Who is already so deeply offended. They must say the Rosary."

Through the prayer of the Rosary untold blessings have been showered down upon all humankind throughout the ages. Through the Rosary today as in past times of peril that have threatened civilization, Mary has again come to save all humankind from the evils that overwhelm us.

But the Rosary is especially most helpful in bringing back home life to its full splendor, by raising the family to a higher family circle where God is Father and Mary is Mother and we are all children of God. The Family Rosary is a practical way to strengthen the unity of family life.

THE WORD OF GOD

"Who is she that comes forth like the morning rising, as beautiful as the moon, as bright as the sun, as awe-inspiring as an army in battle array?"   —Song 6:10

"Listen to me, my faithful children: blossom like roses planted near a stream of water; send out your fragrance like incense, and break forth in blossoms like the lily. Scatter your fragrance and sing a hymn of praise; bless the Lord for all His works."   —Sir 39:13-14

NOVENA PRAYERS

Novena Prayer

MY dearest Mother Mary, behold me, your child, in prayer at your feet. Accept this Holy Rosary, which I offer you in accordance with your requests at Fatima, as a proof of my tender love for you, for the intentions of the Sacred Heart of Jesus, in atonement for the offenses committed against your Immaculate Heart, and for this special favor which I earnestly request in my Rosary Novena: *(Mention your request)*.

I beg you to present my petition to your Divine Son. If you will pray for me, I cannot be refused. I know, dearest Mother, that you want me to seek God's holy Will concerning my request. If what I ask for should not be granted, pray that I may receive that which will be of greater benefit to my soul.

I offer you this spiritual "Bouquet of Roses" because I love you. I put all my confidence in you, since your prayers before God are most powerful. For the greater glory of God and for the sake of Jesus, your loving Son, hear and grant my prayer. Sweet Heart of Mary, be my salvation.

THE HOLY ROSARY

*O*N *the Cross:* In the Name of the Father, etc. I believe in God, the Father Almighty, Creator of heaven and earth; and in Jesus Christ, His only Son, our Lord; Who was conceived by the Holy Spirit, born of the Virgin Mary, suffered under Pontius Pilate, was crucified, died, and was buried. He descended into hell; the third day he arose again from the dead; he ascended into heaven, and sits at the right hand of God, the Father Almighty; from thence he shall come to judge the living and the dead. I believe in the Holy Spirit, the Holy Catholic Church, the Communion of Saints, the forgiveness of sins, the resurrection of the body, and life everlasting. Amen.

On the first large bead: Our Father, etc.

On the next three beads: For an increase of faith, hope, and charity. Hail Mary, etc. (*3 times*).

Glory be to the Father, etc.

Fatima prayer (after each decade): "O my Jesus, forgive us our sins, save us from the fire of hell, take all souls to heaven, and help especially those most in need of Your mercy."

The Five

Joyful

Mysteries

1. The Annunciation
For the love of humility.

Said on Mondays and Saturdays [except during Lent], and the Sundays from Advent to Lent.

2. The Visitation
For charity toward my neighbor.

4. The Presentation
For the virtue of obedience.

3. The Nativity
For the spirit of poverty.

5. Finding in the Temple
For the virtue of piety.

See p. 39 for Prayer after the Rosary.

The Five Luminous Mysteries*

Said on Thursdays [except during Lent].

*Reprinted from our book *Pray the Rosary*, which in 2002 received the Imprimatur from Most Rev. Frank J. Rodimer, Bishop of Paterson.

3. Proclamation of the Kingdom
For seeking God's forgiveness.

1. The Baptism of Jesus
For living my Baptismal Promises.

4. The Transfiguration
Becoming a New Person in Christ.

2. Christ's Self-Manifestation at Cana
For doing whatever Jesus says.

5. Institution of the Eucharist
For active participation at Mass.

See p. 39 for Prayer after the Rosary.

The Five

Sorrowful

Mysteries

1. Agony in the Garden
For true contrition.

Said on Tuesdays and Fridays throughout the year, and every day from Ash Wednesday until Easter.

2. Scourging at the Pillar
For the virtue of purity.

4. Carrying of the Cross
For the virtue of patience.

3. Crowning with Thorns
For moral courage.

5. The Crucifixion
For final perseverance.

See p. 39 for Prayer after the Rosary.

The Five Glorious Mysteries

3. Descent of the Holy Spirit
For love of God.

Said on Wednesdays [except during Lent], and the Sundays from Easter to Advent.

1. The Resurrection
For the virtue of faith.

4. Assumption of the B.V.M.
For devotion to Mary.

2. The Ascension
For the virtue of hope.

5. Crowning of the B.V.M.
For eternal happiness.

See p. 39 for Prayer after the Rosary.

—DECEMBER—

THE IMMACULATE CONCEPTION OF THE BLESSED VIRGIN MARY

(December 8)

MEDITATION

THE Church teaches that from the first moment of her conception the Blessed Virgin Mary possessed sanctifying grace, even the fullness of grace, with the infused virtues and gifts of the Holy Spirit. Yet she remained subject to death and other pains and miseries of life that her Son Himself willed to undergo.

Mary was "in the first instant of her conception, by the singular grace and privilege of the all-powerful God, in virtue of the merits of Jesus Christ, Savior of the human race, preserved from all stain of original sin."

This article of faith is founded upon Scripture and upon the constant Tradition of the Church. Since God Himself had announced from the beginning of the world that Mary was destined "to crush the head" of the infernal serpent through her Divine Son, she could not have begun her life by being wounded herself by his poisonous bite and subject to his power. The Archangel Gabriel called her "full of grace" because she never was deprived of sanctifying grace, and consequently she possessed this grace in the first moment of her conception.

The Fathers and writers of the Church compare Mary to the ark of Noah which alone escaped the universal deluge; to the thornbush which Moses saw burning, but not consumed; to the enclosed garden; to the rod of Aaron which, when laid in the ark, budded and blossomed without having taken root; to the fleece of Gideon which remained dry while the ground all around it became moist with dew. They look upon Mary as the Queen who came from the Most High, perfect, beautiful, and without original sin; as the paradise of innocence which God Himself planted and protected against all the attacks of the poisonous serpent.

Reason, too, approves of Mary's Immaculate Conception, for this privilege corresponds with her sublime vocation. She was the throne of God, the wonderful palace in which the Son of God chose to dwell for nine months. Her womb was the chosen place honored by the mysterious working of the Holy Spirit. If everything that comes in contact with God must be pure and immaculate, purity was necessary for her, the vessel in which the Son of God formed His Flesh and Blood. Her Immaculate Conception is a brilliant witness to the sanctity of Jesus, her Son.

If Jesus, the Son of God, could choose for His Mother her who pleased Him most, He would surely choose one acceptable to the Blessed Trinity and worthy of the great honor for which she was destined. Mary was, therefore not only free from all actual sin, but she also remained exempt from original sin; otherwise, she would not have been a Mother suitable for Jesus Christ, the Son of God.

As Eve received natural life from Adam, Mary received spiritual life, the life of grace, through her Son. If Eve was originally immaculate, Mary, who is superior to Eve in merits, could not be inferior to her in dignity. Since Eve was immaculate in her formation, Mary must have been immaculate in her conception.

God Himself has testified to Mary's Immaculate Conception by miracles. Who can number the wonders that have been wrought at Lourdes, where she appeared eighteen times and declared to Bernadette and to the world: "I am the Immaculate Conception," just four years after this doctrine was defined as a dogma of faith? Mary declared to the whole world her approval of this doctrine and that she was not only immaculately conceived, but that she is the Immaculate Conception.

We should be grateful to God for the grace of Baptism by which we were cleansed from original sin and spiritually regenerated and sanctified. We ought to ask the Immaculate Virgin Mary to guard us against every sin, above all against every mortal sin, lest we lose the grace of God, infinitely greater than all the riches of the world.

The solemn feast of the Immaculate Conception, a Holy Day of Obligation, is celebrated on December 8.

The Immaculate Conception is honored also on the feast of Our Lady of Lourdes, February 11, and in the devotion of the Miraculous Medal.

THE WORD OF GOD

"You are the glory of Jerusalem, you are the joy of Israel, you are the honor of our people. . . . May you be blessed by the Lord Almighty forever and ever."

—Jud 15:9-10

"I will greatly rejoice in the Lord, and my soul shall be joyful in my God. For He has clothed me with a robe of salvation, and He has covered me with a mantle of justice, . . . like a bride adorned with her jewels."   —Isa 61:10

"A great sign appeared in heaven: a woman clothed with the sun, with the moon under her feet, and on her head a crown of twelve stars."   —Rev 12:1

NOVENA PRAYERS

Novena Prayer

IMMACULATE Virgin Mary, you were pleasing in the sight of God from the first moment of your conception in the womb of your mother, St. Anne. You were chosen to be the Mother of Jesus Christ, the Son of God. I believe the teaching of Holy Mother the Church, that in the first instant of your conception, by the singular grace and privilege of Almighty God, in virtue of the merits of Jesus Christ, Savior of the human race and your beloved Son, you were preserved from all stain of original sin. I thank God for this wonderful privilege and grace He bestowed upon you as I honor your Immaculate Conception.

Look graciously upon me as I implore this special favor: *(Mention your request).*

Virgin Immaculate, Mother of God and my Mother, from your throne in heaven turn your eyes of pity upon me. Filled with confidence in your goodness and power, I beg you to help me in this journey of life, which is so full of dangers for my soul. I entrust myself entirely to you, that I may never be the slave of the devil through sin, but may always live a humble and pure life. I consecrate myself to you forever, for my only desire is to love your Divine Son Jesus.

Mary, since none of your devout servants has ever perished, may I, too, be saved. Amen.

A Prayer of Saint Ephrem

BLESSED Virgin, immaculate and pure, you are the sinless Mother of your Son, Who is the mighty Lord of the universe. Since you are holy and inviolate, the hope of the hopeless and sinful, I sing your praises. I praise you as full of every grace, for you bore the God-Man. I venerate you; I invoke you and implore your aid.

Holy and Immaculate Virgin, help me in every need that presses upon me and free me from all the temptations of the devil. Be my intercessor and advocate at the hour of death and judgment. Deliver me from the fire that is not extinguished and from the outer darkness. Make me worthy of the glory of your Son, O dearest and most kind Virgin Mother. You indeed are my most secure and only hope for you are holy in the sight of God, to whom be honor and glory, majesty and power forever. Amen.

Prayer

FATHER, You prepared the Virgin Mary to be the worthy Mother of Your Son. You made it possible for her to share beforehand in the salvation Your Son, Jesus Christ, would bring by His death, and kept her without sin from the first moment of her conception. Give us the grace by her prayers ever to live in Your presence without sin. We ask this through the same Christ our Lord. Amen.

THE MIRACULOUS MEDAL

(December 8)

MEDITATION

THE medal of the Immaculate Conception, commonly called the Miraculous Medal, was manifested to a spiritual daughter of Saint Vincent de Paul, Saint Catherine Labouré. This took place in the chapel of the Motherhouse of the Sisters of Charity, 140 rue du Bac, Paris, France.

Sister Catherine, during her novitiate days, received extraordinary favors from God, such as visions of the heart of Saint Vincent and manifestations of our Lord in the Blessed Sacrament. In 1830 she was blessed with the apparitions of Mary Immaculate to which we owe the Miraculous Medal.

Saint Catherine describes the apparition of our Lady on November 27, 1830, in these words: "Her feet rested on a white globe. I saw rings on her fingers, and each ring was set with gems. The larger gems emitted greater rays and the smaller gems, smaller rays. I could not express what I saw, the beauty and the brilliance of the dazzling rays. A voice said, 'They are the symbols of the graces I shed upon those who ask for them.'

"A frame formed round the Blessed Virgin. Within it was written in letters of gold: 'O Mary, conceived without sin, pray for us who have recourse to you.' Then the voice said, 'Have a Medal struck after this model. All who wear it will receive great graces; they should wear it around the neck.' At this instant the tableau seemed to turn, and I beheld the reverse of the Medal: a large 'M' surmounted by a bar and a cross; beneath the 'M' were the Hearts of Jesus and Mary, the one crowned with thorns, the other pierced with a sword."

When Saint Catherine related the vision to her confessor, he asked her whether she had seen any writing on the back of the Medal. She answered that she had seen none at all. He told her to ask the Blessed Virgin what to put there. The Sister prayed to Mary a long time and one day during meditation she seemed to hear a voice saying, "The 'M' and the two hearts express enough."

The Medal was made according to our Lady's design. It was freely circulated and in a short time was worn by millions. Many graces were given and blessings bestowed until the little Medal of the Immaculate Conception became known by the name it bears today, the Miraculous Medal.

THE WORD OF GOD

"All the words of my mouth are sincere. . . . They are all clear to the person of intelligence and right to those who arrive at knowledge. Take my instruction in preference to silver, and knowledge rather than fine gold."
—Prov 8:8-10

"I love those who love me, and those who diligently look for me find me. Riches and honor are with me, dazzling wealth and prosperity. My fruit is better than gold, even the finest of gold, and my products are better than choice silver."
—Prov 8:17-19

"Children, listen to me: Happy are those who keep my ways. Heed instruction and be wise, and do not refuse it."
—Prov 8:32-33

NOVENA PRAYERS
Opening Prayer

COME, Holy Spirit, fill the hearts of Your faithful, and kindle in them the fire of Your love. Send forth Your Spirit, and they shall be created; and You shall renew the face of the earth.

O God, You instructed the hearts of the faithful by the light of the Holy Spirit. Grant us in the same Spirit to be truly wise and ever to rejoice in His consolation, through Jesus Christ our Lord. Amen.

O Mary, conceived without sin, pray for us who have recourse to you. *(3 times.)*

Lord Jesus Christ, You have been pleased to glorify by numberless miracles the Blessed Virgin Mary, immaculate from the first moment of her conception. Grant that all who devoutly implore her protection on earth may eternally enjoy Your presence in heaven, Who, with the Father and the Holy Spirit, live and reign, God, forever and ever. Amen.

Lord Jesus Christ, for the accomplishment of Your works, You have chosen the weak things of the world, that no flesh may glory in Your sight. And for a better and more widely diffused belief in the Immaculate Conception of Your Mother, You have wished that the Miraculous Medal be manifested to Saint Catherine Labouré. Grant, we beseech You, that filled with like humility, we may glorify this mystery by word and work. Amen.

Memorare

REMEMBER, O most gracious Virgin Mary, that never was it known that anyone who fled to your protection, implored your help, or sought your intercession, was left unaided. Inspired with this confidence, I fly to you, O Virgin of virgins, my Mother. To you I come, before you I stand, sinful and sorrowful. O Mother of the Word Incarnate, despise not my petitions, but in your mercy hear and answer me. Amen.

Novena Prayer

IMMACULATE Virgin Mary, Mother of our Lord Jesus Christ and our Mother, penetrated with the most lively confidence in your all-powerful and never-failing intercession, manifested so often through the Miraculous Medal, we your loving and trustful children implore you to obtain for us the graces and favors we ask during this Novena, if they be beneficial to our immortal souls, and the souls for which we pray: *(Mention your request).*

You know, Mary, how often our souls have been the sanctuaries of your Son Who hates iniquity. Obtain for us then a deep hatred of sin and that purity of heart which will attach us to God alone so that our every thought, word, and deed may tend to His greater glory.

Obtain for us also a spirit of prayer and self-denial that we may recover by penance what we have lost by sin and at length attain to that blessed abode where you are the Queen of Angels and of People. Amen.

Act of Consecration

VIRGIN Mother of God, Mary Immaculate, we dedicate and consecrate ourselves to you under the title of Our Lady of the Miraculous Medal. May this Medal be a sure sign of your affection for us and a constant reminder of our duties toward you. Ever while wearing it, may we be blessed by your loving protection and preserved in the grace of your Son.

Most powerful Virgin, Mother of our Savior, keep us close to you every moment of our lives. Obtain for us, your children, the grace of a happy death; so that, in union with you, we may enjoy the blessing of heaven forever. Amen.

Mary, conceived without sin, pray for us who have recourse to you. *(3 times.)*

OUR LADY OF GUADALUPE

(December 12)

MEDITATION

ACCORDING to tradition the Blessed Virgin appeared to a fifty-five-year-old Aztec Indian Juan Diego, who was hurrying to Mass in Mexico City, on Saturday, December 9, 1531. She sent him to Bishop Zumaraga to ask that a church be built on the spot where she stood. She was at the same place that evening and Sunday evening to get the bishop's answer. After cross-questioning Juan, the bishop ordered him to ask for a sign from the lady who had said she was the Mother of God.

Mary spoke to Juan in these words: "Know and take heed, my dear little son, that I am the holy Mary, ever Virgin, Mother of the true God for Whom we live, the Creator of all the world, Maker of heaven and earth. I urgently desire that a church should be built here, to bear witness to my love, my compassion, my help and protection, For I am a merciful Mother to you and to all your people who love me and trust in me and invoke my help."

Our Lady would give the bishop a sign. She told Juan to go up to the rocks and gather roses. He knew it was neither the time nor the place for roses, but he obeyed. Gathering the roses into the long cloak worn by Mexican Indians, he returned to the Blessed Mother who arranged them. When he arrived at the bishop's home, Juan unfolded his cloak and the roses fell out. Startled to see the bishop and his attendants kneeling before him, he looked at the cloak and saw there the figure of the Virgin Mary, just as he had described her. The picture was venerated in the bishop's chapel and soon after carried in procession to the first church.

The picture that has aroused all this devotion is a representation of the Immaculate Conception, with the sun, moon, and stars, according to the text in the Book of Revelation. Mary, clothed in a blue robe dotted with stars, stands on the crescent moon. Underneath the crescent is a supporting Angel. The rays of the sun shoot out on all sides from behind the Blessed Mother.

In 1709, a rich and beautiful shrine was erected near Mexico City; in 1904, it was made a basilica and contains the picture. Pilgrimages have been made to this shrine almost uninterruptedly since 1531. A new and much larger basilica was recently completed. Twenty Popes favored the shrine and its tradition.

The apparition of Our Lady of Guadalupe is Mary's only recorded appearance in North America.

Pope Pius XII said, "We are certain that so long as you—Our Lady of Guadalupe—are recognized as Queen and Mother, America and Mexico are saved." He proclaimed her the Patroness of the Americas. The United States was dedicated to the Immaculate Conception by the Third Plenary Council of Baltimore in 1846.

The Image of Our Lady of Guadalupe is the image of the Immaculate Conception. As patroness of Pan-American unity, Our Lady of Guadalupe influences her children to turn toward one another in common love for her and her beloved Son. Because of the close link between the Church in Mexico and the Church in the United States this feast is also celebrated in the United States on December 12.

THE WORD OF GOD

"I have chosen and sanctified this place, that my name may be there forever, and my eyes and my heart may be there perpetually."   —2 Chr 7:16

"You are beautiful . . . , O My love, as comely as Jerusalem, as awe-inspiring as an army in battle array."
—Song 6:4

"Who is she that comes forth like the morning rising, as beautiful as the moon, as bright as the sun, as awe-inspiring as an army in battle array?"   —Song 6:10

NOVENA PRAYERS
Novena Prayer

OUR Lady of Guadalupe, according to your message in Mexico I venerate you as "the Virgin Mother of the true God for Whom we live, the Creator of all the world, Maker of heaven and earth." In spirit I kneel before your most holy Image which you miraculously imprinted upon the cloak of the Indian Juan Diego, and with the faith of the countless numbers of pilgrims who visit your shrine, I beg you for this favor: *(Mention your request)*.

Remember, O Immaculate Virgin, the words you spoke to your devout client, "I am a merciful Mother to you and to all your people who love me and trust in me and invoke my help. I listen to their lamentations and solace all their sorrows and their sufferings." I beg you to be a merciful Mother to me, because I sincerely love you and trust in you and invoke your help.

I entreat you, Our Lady of Guadalupe, to grant my request, if this should be the Will of God, in order that I may "bear witness to your love, your compassion, your help and protection." Do not forsake me in my needs.

Our Lady of Guadalupe, pray for us. Hail Mary *(3 times)*.

Prayer by Pope John Paul II

O IMMACULATE Virgin, Mother of the true God and Mother of the Church! You, who from this place reveal your clemency and your pity to all those who ask for your protection; hear the prayer that we address to you with filial trust, and present it to your Son Jesus, our sole Redeemer.

Mother of mercy, Teacher of hidden and silent sacrifice, to you, who come to meet us sinners, we dedicate on this day all our being and all our love. We also dedicate to you our life, our work, our joys, our infirmities and our sorrows.

Grant peace, justice, and prosperity to our people; for we entrust to your care all that we have and all that we are, Our Lady and Mother.

We wish to be entirely yours and to walk with you along the way of complete faithfulness to Jesus Christ in His Church: hold us always with your loving hand.

Virgin of Guadalupe, Mother of the Americas, we pray to you for all the Bishops, that they may lead the faithful along paths of intense Christian life, of love and humble service of God and souls.

Contemplate this immense harvest, and intercede with the Lord that He may instill a hunger for holiness in the whole People of God, and grant abundant vocations of priests and religious, strong in the faith and zealous dispensers of God's mysteries.

Grant to our homes the grace of loving and respecting life in its beginnings, with the same love with which you conceived in your womb the life of the Son of God.

Blessed Virgin Mary, Mother of Fair Love, protect our families, so that they may always be united, and bless the upbringing of our children.

Our hope, look upon us with compassion, teach us to go continually to Jesus and, if we fall, help us to rise again, to return to Him, by means of the confession of our faults and sins in the Sacrament of Penance, which gives peace to the soul. We beg you to grant us a great love for all the holy Sacraments, which are, as it were, the signs that your Son left us on earth.

Thus, Most Holy Mother, with the peace of God in our conscience, with our hearts free from evil and hatred, we will be able to bring to all true joy and true peace, which come to us from your Son, our Lord Jesus Christ, Who with God the Father and the Holy Spirit, lives and reigns forever. Amen.

Mexico, January 1979

Prayer

GOD of power and mercy, You blessed the Americas at Tepeyac with the presence of the Virgin Mary at Guadalupe. May her prayers help all men and women to accept each other as brothers and sisters. Through Your justice present in our hearts may Your peace reign in the world. We ask this through our Lord Jesus Christ, Your Son, Who lives and reigns with You and the Holy Spirit, one God, forever and ever. Amen.